BARBECUE COOKBOOK

Tasty and Easy to Follow Recipes to Grill

Your Favorite Foods

SHARMA POHL

Table of Contents

Anthelme Brillat-Savarin

The discovery of a new dish does more for the happiness of the human race than the discovery of a star

INTRODUCTION

Everyone, anywhere these days, has a favorite grilling method, specialized grill, or cookbook. Still, the result is almost always the same: moist, smoky, tasty meat and vegetables grilled over an open flame. The act of lighting a grill brings us to our past, encourages us to appreciate the outdoors, and reconnects us with our inner cave dwellers. For the perfect backyard

1

BBQ, you don't need any machine or high-end device; all you need is a basic barbecue, some meat, and a couple of techniques up your sleeve.

Grilling is a dry heat cooking technique that uses clear, radiant heat. It allows you to cook meat and vegetables in a short amount of time, which is ideal for every night of the week.

Cooking on a grill uses a phenomenon known as thermal radiation. The heat source may be above or below what's being grilled, but when it's above the food, it's generally referred to as "broiled." The majority of grills get their heat from below. It can be either gas or charcoal.

In the present-day world, whenever you go to a restaurant, grilled food tops on the menu. It's what everyone enjoys despite of variating culture, age, social class, etc.

In the present times, grilled food is considered the festive food that is prepared for the community. It is mostly cooked outside and is the focal point of the social functions.

Cooking grilled food in everyday life is not hard. It is an easy and fast way of cooking that helps to preserve the nutrients of the food. Any rookie chef can do it. All you need is the basic techniques and your favorite protein.

This book provides a brief introduction to grilling, and gives detailed recipes that you can try at home and become a host to BBQ backyard parties.

CHAPTER 01

TYPES
OF GRILLS

CHAPTER 1 - TYPES OF GRILLS

A variety of ways classify the world's thousands, if not dozens, of distinct grills. You may categorize them based on the type of fuel they use, such as wood-burning grills, gas grills, and charcoal grills. You may group them by areas of origin, such as South American grills or Southeast Asian grills. However, from the perspective of a griller, the most functional method is to arrange the fire and position the food for frying. It is what decides the temperature at which the food can grill and how easily it can cook. Understanding and monitoring these factors can determine how effective you are as a grill master..

1.1   Vessel Grill

The term coined to define thick-walled, deep ceramic grills that cook food using both radiant heats from the sidewalls and direct warmth from the coals. Instead of using a grill grate, food is often grilled directly on the walls or on a perpendicular spit located within the firebox.

Iran's tandoor, India's tandoor, and kamado cookers are all examples.

Roasting at high temperatures, smoking and grilling are all possible with the kamado cooker.

Flatbreads, such as Indian naan that are cooked directly on the tandoor's walls, are best suited for these types of grills. On a vertical spit, kebabs, ham, fish steaks, tiny lamb and goat wings, peppers, and paneer cheese are all grilled.

1.2 Smoker Grill

While smoking is one of the oldest ways of cooking and storing foods, the smoker as a mobile backyard barbecue grill is a twentieth-century North American innovation. Grilling is practiced all around the world, but not all grill societies burn.

Included are Texas offset barrel smokers, box smokers from North America, China, and Europe, upright water smokers, and pellet/sawdust smokers from North America (such as the Traeger and Bradley).

Smoking, indirect grilling of wood smoke at low to moderate temperatures foodstuffs, are ideally suited for these grills.

It is adequate to cook foods like the rough, tasty cuts of beef like ribs and brisket.

1.3   Rotisserie Grill

This grill brings movement to the often-stagnant grilling method. A turnspit's steady, gentle rotating level out the cooking period, baste the meat, melt fat, and brown the outside. Foods that are spit-roasted come out fresh on the exterior and juicy on the inside.

Included under this category are Tuscany's and Germany's wood rotisseries, France's gas wall rotisseries, Malaysia's and Singapore's charcoal chicken wing rotisseries, and the infrared ones incorporated into American gas grills. Grill masters use vertical rotisseries to render Turkish doner, Greek gyro, and Middle Eastern shawarma in the eastern Mediterranean and the Middle East.

Ideally used for combining the benefits of both indirect and direct grilling. The food directly faces the heat, much as in the direct grilling, except in indirect grilling, the food is cooked adjoining, rather than directly above the flames.

Cylindrical and fatty ingredients, such as entire poultry, chicken wings, pigs, whole hogs, and rib roasts, work best with this grill

1.4   Open Pit and Campfire Grills

Grilling (or cooking) used to be performed over or adjoining to a campfire rather than on a grill. This ancient method is still widely used, particularly in America.

Included under this category are Argentina's Asado and Brazil's Fogo de Cho—meats grilled in front of a fire—typify open-pit grilling. The Pacific Northwest's salmon "bakes," Connecticut's planked shad, and roasting marshmallows on sticks to produce s'mores are all examples of campfire grilling. Radiant-heat roasting is what it's used for.

Whole calf, pig, goat, and tuna, skin-on salmon fillets, and beef ribs are the best choices to be cooked on these types of grills.

1.5   Open Grills

The most basic of all grills is a stone or metal box with a wood, charcoal, or propane fire at the bottom and food directly over the fire. The grill grate is not needed.

Table grills from North America and Europe, South American parrillas, the Balkan mangal, the Italian fogolar, Indonesian saté grills, Asian bucket grills, and the Australian flattop grill are only a few examples.

It is ideally used for direct grilling on high heat.

Kebabs, Satés, steaks, cuts, fish fillets, veggies, and other tiny, fresh, speedily foods are perfect for cooking using these grills.

1.6   Closed Grills

When you combine an open grill with a tall lid that you can lift and drop, you have a covered grill. This could seem to be a minor advancement, but the closed grill allows you to incorporate two more essential live-fire cooking techniques into your oeuvre: indirect grilling and smoking.

The gas grill, kettle grill, and 55-gallon steel-drum grill are all included under this category.

Larger or thicker items may be directly grilled on this grill. Grilling and vaping done in an indirect manner are ideally suited for this.

Foods that go well with this type of grilling include beef and fish steaks, as well Meats with higher fat content, such as double-thick veal, pork chops, pork back ribs, pork shoulder, and also entire duck and chicken.

CHAPTER 02

VEGETABLES AND SIDES RECIPES

CHAPTER 2 - VEGETABLES AND SIDES RECIPES

2.1 CHILI-RUBBED JICAMA STEAKS WITH QUESO FRESCO

Ready in about: 20 minutes - Servings: 2 - Difficulty: easy

Ingredients:

- 1 tsp. of chili powder.

- 1 lb. jicama, peeled and cut into half-inch-thick slices.

- Lime wedges for serving.

- 1 tbsp. of neutral oil, like grapeseed or corn.

- Salt and black pepper.

- 4 oz. of crumbled queso fresco cheese.

Instructions:

1. Preheat a charcoal or gas grill to medium-high heat and place the rack about 4 inches from the blaze. In a big mixing bowl, combine the oil, chili powder, and a pinch of salt and pepper. Toss in the jicama until uniformly covered.

2. Place the jicama on the grill and cook for 2 minutes, or until golden brown. Allow to grill for another 2 to 3 minutes after turning the slices and adding the queso fresco. With lime wedges, serve hot or at room temperature.

2.2 TERIYAKI CABBAGE STEAKS

Ready in about: 1 hour - Servings: 6 - Difficulty: hard

Ingredients:

- ½ cup of mirin—or ¼ cup of honey mixed with ¼ cup of water.

- 1 tsp. of minced garlic.

- 1 small cabbage cored and cut crosswise into one and a half-inch-thick slices.

- Half cup of soy sauce.

- 1 tbsp. of minced fresh ginger.

- 2 tbsp. of chopped scallions.

- 2 tbsp. of neutral oil, like grapeseed or corn.

- Lemon wedges for serving.

- Salt and black pepper.

Instructions:

1. Heat a charcoal or gas grill to a medium-high temperature, leaving a section of the grill cool for indirect grilling, and place the rack about 4-inches from the blaze. In a shallow saucepan over medium-low heat, mix the soy sauce and mirin and simmer for 2 to 3 minutes, or until the mixture starts to bubble. Take the pan off the heat and stir in the garlic, ginger, and scallions.

2. Oil the cabbage slices and season with pepper and salt. Close the grill cover and position the cabbage on the cool side of the grill. Cook for 40 to 45 minutes, testing and turning regularly until leaves are quickly pierced with a sharp knife. Brush the cabbage liberally with the teriyaki mixture and transfer it to the cooler portion of the grill until it is soft. Cook for 3 to 5 minutes, rotating once or twice and brushing with more of the sauce until it's browned.

3. Serve the cabbage hot or warm with lemon wedges and any leftover teriyaki sauce.

2.3 VIETNAMESE-STYLE PORTOBELLO MUSHROOMS

Ready in about: 20 minutes - Servings: 4 - Difficulty: easy

Ingredients:

- ¼ cup of fresh lime juice.

- 1 fresh seeded and minced hot red chili.

- ½ tsp. of sugar.

- 4 large portobello mushrooms, stem removed.

- ¼ cup of peanut oil.

- 2 tbsp. of chopped fresh mint, plus more for garnish.

- 1 tbsp. of fish sauce.

- Salt and lots of black pepper as per your taste.

Instructions:

1. 1Heat a gas charcoal grill to high heat, then place the rack 4 inches from the blaze. Combine the oil, juice, mint, chili, sugar, and fish sauce in a mixing bowl and season to taste with pepper and salt. Around half of this mixture can be rubbed all over the mushrooms.

2. Grill the mushrooms with the tops of their caps facing away from the blaze for 5 to 8 minutes or before they tend to tan. Turn and brush with the remaining marinade. 5 to 10 minutes more on the grill before tender and well browned all over. Serve hot, warm, or at room temperature, garnished with more mint.

2.4 CHARRED PEPPERS

Ready in about: 1 hour and 20 minutes - Servings: 6 - Difficulty: hard

Ingredients:

- 2 or so tbsp. of olive oil.
- Fresh lemon juice, capers, or anchovies (optional)
- 12 or more long peppers, red, green or both.
- Salt (optional)

Instructions:

1. Make a roaring fire. Wood is best, but charcoal is a close second. There can be no more than 3 or 4 inches between the rack and the fire, and peppers should be added only when the flames begin to die down; there would be no flare-up.

2. Place peppers on the grill in a single layer to avoid overcrowding. Turn them as they blacken to ensure that they char on all or almost all surfaces. Move them to a bowl where you can pile them up when they end.

3. Allow cooling. Peel and seed the peppers, rinsing the residual seeds and skin with as little water as practicable. But don't go overboard: a few seeds and scraps of skin would suffice. Often, the closest the peppers are to being entire, the more appealing they are.

4. Serve with a drizzle of olive oil and a touch of salt, if necessary. Capers and anchovies, as well as lemon juice, aren't likely to harm. These would hold for at least a week in the refrigerator.

2.5 POTATO FONDANTES WITH OREGANO

Ready in about: 40 minutes - Servings: 6 - Difficulty: moderate

Ingredients:

- 1 ½ tbsp. of unsalted butter.

- 3 lb. of medium potatoes.

- 2 tbsp. of canola oil.

- ½ tsp. of salt.

- 3 tbsp. of coarsely chopped fresh oregano.

Instructions

1. Remove some eyes and dark marks; just don't peel the potatoes. In a wide (ideally 10-inch) non-stick skillet, split potatoes in half lengthwise and place cut side down in 1 sheet.

2. Transfer 1 ½ cups water, oil, butter, oregano, and salt to the pot. Get the mixture to a boil over high pressure, then switch off the heat. Reduce the heat to medium and continue to cook for another 20 to 25 minutes. By this time, the water should have evaporated, and the potatoes should be well browned in butter and oil.

3. Flip the potatoes over and brown them gently on the other side for 2 or 3 minutes.

2.6 GRILLED MUSHROOM ANTIPASTO SALAD

Ready in about: 40 minutes - Servings: 4 to 6 - Difficulty: moderate

Ingredients:

- 7 tbsp. of extra-virgin olive oil, divided.

- 2 tbsp. of Champagne vinegar or white wine vinegar.

- 1 tsp. of dried oregano.

- 2 oz. Parmesan shaved.

- ¼ cup of drained Peppadew peppers in brine, coarsely chopped.

- 2 lb. assorted mushrooms, wiped clean, trimmed, torn into big pieces if large.

- Kosher salt.

- 1 tsp. of Aleppo-style pepper.

- 1 garlic clove, finely grated.

- ½ cup of Castelvetrano olives, coarsely chopped.

Instructions:

1. 1Heat a grill to extreme temperatures. In a wide mixing bowl, toss the mushrooms with 3 tbsp. of oil. Let it grill for 2 to 6 minutes, rotating periodically with tongs until slightly charred. Season it with salt and return to the cup.

2. In a shallow bowl, whisk together the Aleppo-style pepper, vinegar, garlic, oregano, and the remaining 4 tbsp. of oil; season with black pepper and salt. Toss the mushrooms in the sauce to seal them. Toss in the olives, Parmesan, and Peppadew peppers once well combined. Then serve after combining everything.

2.7 GRILLED POTATO SALAD WITH CHILES AND BASIL

Ready in about: 40 minutes - Servings: 4 - Difficulty: moderate

Ingredients:

- ½ cup of kosher salt, plus more.

- 3 tbsp. of fish sauce.

- ¼ cup plus 3 tbsp. of extra-virgin olive oil, plus more for drizzling.

- 1 large red onion.

- 2 cups of basil leaves.

- 2 lb. baby Yukon Gold potatoes.

- ⅔ cup of unseasoned rice vinegar.

- 1 tbsp. of honey.

- 2 red Fresno chilies, thinly sliced.

- 3 garlic cloves.

- 2 tbsp. of toasted sesame seeds.

Instructions:

1. In a big saucepan, cover potatoes with 3 quarts of water. With half cup of salt, stir it in over medium-high pressure, bring to a boil. Reduce heat to medium-low and proceed to cook for another 12 minutes or until potatoes are only soft when stabbed with a skewer or paring knife. Drain and set aside to cool.

2. Meanwhile, preheat the grill to medium. In a shallow bowl, combine the vinegar, honey, fish sauce, and 3 tbsp. of oil. Add the chilies and mix well. Put aside the dressing after seasoning it with salt.

3. Break the onion in half through the base, then cut half into 5 wedges, keeping the root in place.

4. In a broad mixing cup, finely grind the garlic. With ¼ cup of oil whisked in Toss, the onion wedges into the mixing bowl. When you add the potatoes to the dish, softly smash them with your hands and toss gently to cover them in garlic oil. Season with salt and pepper.

5. Put for 12 to 15 minutes on the fire, rotating periodically, before potatoes and onion wedges are charred all over. When the onions and the potatoes are done grilling, clean out the bowl you used to throw them in, then add them to it.

6. Toss the potatoes in the dressing to cover them. Add basil and sesame seeds, tearing some large leaves in half. Taste and adjust the seasoning with salt if necessary, then mix to blend.

7. In a serving dish, position the potato salad. Drizzle some oil on top.

CHAPTER 03

BURGERS RECIPES

CHAPTER 3 - BURGERS RECIPES

3.1   BEEF TARTARE BURGER

Ready in about: 30 minutes - Servings: 4 - Difficulty: easy

Ingredients:

- 1 peeled shallot.

- 1 tbsp. of capers.

- ½ cup of chopped fresh parsley.

- 2 tsp. of Worcestershire sauce.

- 1 ½ lb. of chuck or fatty sirloin.

- 1 medium peeled clove of garlic.

- 2 anchovy fillets.

- ½ tsp. of Tabasco sauce.

- Salt and pepper according to taste.

- Lemon slices for garnish (optional).

- Chopped cooked egg, capers, whole anchovies, sweet white onion, fresh parsley

Instructions:

1. The grill rack should be about 4 inches from the flame, and the flame should be medium to high. In a food processor, pulse the beef, garlic, shallot, anchovies, and capers, if using, until roughly ground—not much finer than sliced.

2. Combine it with Worcestershire sauce, parsley, and in a mixing bowl, and Tabasco sauce season with pepper and salt. Gently combine, then taste it and change seasonings as required. Shape the beef into 4 or more burgers, using as little pressure as possible to prevent compressing it.

3. Grill for 3 minutes per side and another minute per side for each level of doneness after that.

4. If needed, top with chopped capers, egg, anchovies, parsley, onion, and lemon.

3.2   THE PERFECT BASIC BURGER

Ready in about: 35 minutes - Servings: 4 - Difficulty: easy

Ingredients:

- ½ tsp. of salt.

- 1 egg.

- ½ tsp. of ground black pepper.

- ½ cup of fine dry bread crumbs.

- 1 lb. of ground beef.

Instructions

1. Preheat the outdoor grill to high heat and spray the grate gently with oil.

2. Whisk together the egg, pepper, and salt in a medium mixing bowl. Combine the ground beef with the bread crumbs in a mixing bowl. Mix with your hands or a fork until everything is well mixed. Make 4 patties, each around 3/4-inch wide.

3. Place the patties on the grill that has been preheated. Cook for 6 to 8 minutes per side or until ideal doneness is reached.

3.3   CURRY-SPICED LAMB BURGERS

Ready in about: 20 minutes - Servings: 4 - Difficulty: easy

Ingredients:

- 1 medium (or half large) onion, chopped.

- 1 tsp. of ground coriander.

- ½ tsp. of turmeric.

- Diced mango, red onion, green and red bell pepper, and scallion.

- Lettuce and shredded carrot for garnish (optional).

- 1 ½ lb. of boneless lamb shoulder, cut into chunks.

- 1 fresh chili, seeded and minced.

- 1 tsp. of ground cumin.

- Salt and black pepper according to taste.

Instructions:

1. The heat is supposed to be set to medium-high, and the rack should be about 4-inches away from the flames. Place the onion and lamb in a food processor and process until coarsely ground. Add the chili, coriander, turmeric, and cumin to a bowl and season with pepper and salt. Mix when well, with as minimal handling of the meat as possible. Season with pepper and salt as per the taste. Shape the meat into 4 burgers, using as little pressure to prevent compressing it.

2. Grill for 3 minutes per side or more, until the level of doneness of your preference.

3. If needed, garnish with red and green peppers, diced mango, scallion, and red onion, as well as lettuce and shredded carrot.

3.4 GRILLED CHILI BURGER

Ready in about: 40 minutes. - Servings: 8 - Difficulty: moderate

Ingredients:

- Salt and freshly ground pepper according to taste.

- 1 tsp. of chili powder, or more to taste.

- 4 tsp. of butter, at room temperature.

- 2 lb. of twice-ground round steak.

- 1 finely minced clove of garlic.

- ¼ cup of bread crumbs.

Instructions:

1. Build a charcoal fire. The fire is ready when the coals are hot, and white ash has formed.

2. Combine the meat and the remaining materials in a mixing bowl. Make 8 patties out of the mixture.

3. Grill on both sides when finished to your liking. Serve with relishes on hamburger buns.

3.5   JAPANESE BURGERS WITH WASABI KETCHUP

Ready in about: 30 minutes. - Servings: 4 - Difficulty: easy

Ingredients:

For the wasabi ketchup:

- 2 tbsp. of soy sauce.
- ½ cup of ketchup.

- 1 tbsp. of wasabi paste.

For the burgers:

- ¼ cup of whole milk.
- ½ lb. of ground pork.
- 1 ½ tsp. of soy sauce.
- ¼ tsp. of pepper.
- 4 brioche buns for serving.
- ½ cup panko or other dry bread crumbs.

- ½ lb. of ground sirloin.
- ¼ cup of finely chopped white onion.
- ½ tsp. of salt.
- Sesame oil for coating hands.

Instructions:

1. Whisk together ketchup, wasabi paste, and soy sauce to make the wasabi ketchup.

2. To render the burgers, preheat the grill to medium-high heat. Combine panko and milk in a big mixing bowl and set aside for 2 to 3 minutes.

3. Combine the sirloin, onion, pork, soy sauce, pepper, and salt in a large mixing cup. Knead the meat until it is moist and sticks together, then break it into 4 portions.

4. Apply a light coating of sesame oil to your palms. Roll each piece of meat into a ball with your fingertips, and pat the ball flat with your hands to create a half-inch-thick patty. To prevent the patty from puffing up when grilling, make a small indentation in the middle with the side of your palm.

5. Grill burgers for 10 minutes, turning twice until browned and cooked through with no pink in the center. Allow for a 2-minute rest period. Serve on buns with wasabi ketchup on the side.

3.6   PORTOBELLO MUSHROOM BURGER

Ready in about: 20 minutes - Servings: 4 - Difficulty: easy

Ingredients:

- Extra-virgin olive oil for drizzling.

- 4 large portobello mushrooms.

- Balsamic vinegar, for drizzling.

- Sea salt and freshly ground black pepper.

- Tamari, for drizzling.

For serving:

- Lettuce.

- Sliced red onion.

- 4 hamburger buns, warmed or toasted.

- Sliced tomato.

- Pickles.

- Pesto, Guacamole, or Chipotle Sauce, optional.

- Ketchup, mayo, mustard.

Instructions:

1. Remove the stems from the mushrooms and wipe the caps clean with a wet cloth or paper towel. Drizzle olive oil, tamari, balsamic vinegar, salt, and pepper over the mushrooms on a rimmed plate. Use your hands to coat all sides of the mushrooms.

2. Over medium fire, preheat a grill or grill plate. Place the mushrooms on the grill pan, gill side up. Cook for 5 to 7 minutes on either side or until the mushrooms are soft.

3. Place the mushrooms on the buns and finish with your preferred toppings.

3.7 JUICY HAMBURGERS

Ready in about: 35 minutes - Servings: 8 - Difficulty: easy

Ingredients:

- 1 beaten egg.

- 1 cup of dry bread crumbs.

- 2 tbsp. of Worcestershire sauce.

- 3 tbsp. of evaporated milk.

- 2 lb. of ground beef.

- 2 cloves of garlic, minced.

- 1/8 tsp. of cayenne pepper.

Instructions:

1. Preheat the grill to high.

2. Mix the egg, bread crumbs, ground beef, evaporated milk, cayenne pepper, Worcestershire sauce, and garlic together in a big mixing bowl with your fingertips. Make 8 hamburger patties out of the mixture.

3. Brush oil on the grill grate gently. Grill the burger patties for about 5 minutes a side or until well baked.

POULTRY RECIPES

CHAPTER 4 - POULTRY RECIPES

4.1 CHICKEN BREASTS MARINATED IN BASIL OIL WITH TOMATO AND RED ONION SALAD

Ready in about: 40 minutes (Basil oil excluded) - Servings: 4 - Difficulty: easy

Ingredients:

For basil oil:

- 2 cups plus 7 tbsp. of extra virgin olive oil.
- 2 bunches of fresh basil stems on.

For chicken:

- 4 tsp. of basil oil.
- 1 thinly sliced red onion.
- 12 fresh basil leaves, cut across into thin strips.
- 4 boneless, skinless chicken breast halves.
- 2 large, thinly sliced tomatoes.
- Salt and freshly ground pepper to taste.

Instructions:

For basil oil:

1. A big pot of water should be brought to a boil. 30 seconds after adding the basil, blanch it for 30 seconds. Drain and scrub until cool under cold running water. Drain and thoroughly rinse basil. Add 5 tbsp. of olive oil to a food processor and process until it's smooth. Scrape the mixture into a clean glass container and add 2 cups of olive oil. Shake well before storing for 1 to 2 days in a cool and dry place.

. Using a fine-mesh sieve, strain the oil. To dampen a coffee filter, pour the remaining 2 tsp. of olive oil into it. Place the filter inside the clean glass jar's bottom. Cover the filter with basil oil and let it drip into a container. Continue pouring and letting the oil trickle into the filter until all of it has soaked through. It should be kept in the refrigerator.

For chicken:

1. 1 tsp. basil oil, apply it with a brush to chicken breasts. Allow for half an hour of resting time. Prepare a grill by preheating it. Grill for around 4 to 5 minutes every side on the grill before the chicken is cooked through. Chicken should be sliced and brushed with 1 tsp. of oil.

2. In the middle of all the 4 bowls, place half of the onions and tomatoes. Then pour ¼ tsp. of basil oil over each one and season with pepper and salt. Layers can be repeated. Chicken slices can be fanned out throughout the salad. Sprinkle basil strips on top of the chicken and salad.

4.2 GRILLED BACON-WRAPPED CHICKEN TENDERS

Ready in about: 40 minutes - Servings: 4 - Difficulty: easy

Ingredients:

- 1 tbsp. of BBQ rub.
- 8 chicken tenders.
- 8 slices center cut bacon.
- 1 tsp. of water.
- 2 tbsp. of honey.

Instructions:

1. Preheat the grill to medium heat and spray the grate gently with oil.

2. Rub BBQ rub on chicken. Wrap 2 bacon strips around each tender, tucking the ends in to protect.

3. In a tiny bowl, mix water and honey. Then set aside.

4. Reduce the heat to medium-low temperature and put the chicken tenders on the grill. Close the lid and then grill for around 15 minutes, flipping every 3 minutes until the bacon changes its color to brown and the chicken reaches an inside temperature of 165° F. Increase the heat for the last 2 minutes of cooking for crispier bacon.

5. Place the tenders on a low heat setting and brush with the honey mixture. Serve directly on a tray.

4.3 GRILLED CHICKEN WITH MEDITERRANEAN FLAVORS

Ready in about: 45 minutes - Servings: 4 - Difficulty: moderate

Ingredients:

- 1 tsp. of thyme leaves.

- ½ tsp. of chopped lavender leaves.

- Extra virgin olive oil as needed.

- 8 bay leaves.

- Salt and freshly ground black pepper.

- 1 tsp. of chopped rosemary leaves.

- ¼ cup of roughly chopped parsley.

- 8 chicken drumsticks or thighs.

- 2 lemons, cut into quarters.

Instructions:

1. Light a wood fire or charcoal, or switch on the gas grill. The fire should only be reasonably high, and the rack should be 4 to 6 inches away from the heat source.

2. Integrate pepper, salt, rosemary, thyme, parsley, and lavender in a shallow cup. To create a paste, apply sufficiently olive oil to make a paste. Loosen the skin of the chicken and slip a bay leaf between the skin and the meat, then stuff a part of the herb mixture between the skin and the meat. Return the skin to the meat and season with pepper and salt.

3. Place the chicken skin side up on the grill's coolest section. Turn the chicken over after the fat has melted a little. Shift the chicken to the hottest section of the grill after around 20 minutes, brush with olive oil, and grill until the meat is cooked and the skin is well browned.

4. Serve with lemon wedges on the side.

4.4 GRILLED CHICKEN WITH CHIPOTLE SAUCE

Ready in about: 45 minutes. - Servings: 4 - Difficulty: moderate

Ingredients:

- 1 medium-sized chopped white onion.

- 2 cups of cored and chopped tomatoes.

- 8 chicken thighs, whole legs, or drumsticks.

- 2 tbsp. of lard or neutral oil, like canola or corn.

- 2 dried chipotle chilies, as per your taste.

- Salt and pepper as per taste.

- 2 cloves of garlic halved.

- Lime wedges.

- Freshly chopped cilantro leaves.

Instructions:

1. Preheat a gas grill or start a charcoal or wood fire; the fire should be relatively high, with part of the grill cooler than the rest and the rack 4 to 6 inches from the heat source.

2. In a medium saucepan or skillet, melt the lard or oil over medium flame. When the pan is heated, add the onion and cook, stirring regularly, until it starts to brown, around 5 to 10 minutes. Stir in the tomatoes, chilies, and half a cup of water. Shift the heat such that the mixture simmers slowly and gradually. Cook for 15 minutes, stirring regularly until the chilies are soft and the tomatoes have broken up. If required, season with pepper and salt. When the chipotle sauce is ready, let it cool for a few minutes before cutting the stems and pureeing the mixture in a blender.

3. Meanwhile, rub the chicken with the cut side of garlic cloves, drizzle with oil, and season with pepper and salt to taste.

4. Place the chicken skin side up on the grill's coolest section. Turn the chicken over after the fat has made a little. Shift the chicken to the hottest section of the grill after around 20 minutes. Brush all sides of the chicken with chipotle sauce when it's almost cooked, then simmer for another minute or 2. Serve with cilantro and lime wedges on the side.

4.5 GAYLORD'S TANDOORI CHICKEN

Ready in about: 45 minutes - Servings: 4 to 8 - Difficulty: moderate

Ingredients:

- 2 cups of plain yogurt.

- ½ tsp. of freshly ground black pepper.

- ¼ tsp. of ground cloves.

- 1 tsp. of grated fresh ginger or a ½ tsp. of dried ginger.

- ⅛ to ¼ tsp. of cayenne pepper.

- ½ tsp. of ground cardamom.

- 1 whole chicken (3-4 lb.)

- ½ tsp. of ground cumin.

- ¼ tsp. of freshly grated nutmeg.

- ½ tsp. of ground coriander.

- 1 clove garlic, minced.

- Salt as per taste.

- ½ cup of chopped white onion.

- ½ tsp. of loosely packed saffron threads, or ¼ tsp. of powdered saffron.

- 2 tbsp. of milk.

Instructions:

1. Every chicken's tiny wingtips should be cut off and discarded. Take the skin off the chicken with your fingertips and discard it.

2. Create short gashes through the grain on both sides of chicken breast and legs with a small knife.

3. Take yogurt, black pepper, cumin, nutmeg, coriander, cloves, ginger, cayenne pepper, garlic, cardamom, salt to taste, onion and mix in a food processor. Get a fine liquid out of it.

4. Apply the mixture to the chicken. Switch the chicken over and cover both edges. Refrigerate for at least 24 hours after covering.

5. 1 hour before serving, remove the chicken from the yogurt mixture.

6. Preheat the oven to 500° F. A barbecue grill should be preheated.

7. In a tiny saucepan, heat the milk and add the saffron. Take the pan off the heat and set it aside for 10 minutes.

8. Using a spoon, uniformly distribute the saffron mixture over the chicken.

9. Heavy-duty foil can be used to line a baking dish. Place the chicken with breast facing up.

10. Bake for 20 minutes in the oven.

11. Chicken can be cut into serving sections. Place them on the grill and cook them for a few minutes on both sides.

4.6 GRILLED TABASCO CHICKEN

Ready in about: 40 minutes - Servings: 6 - Difficulty: moderate

Ingredients:

- 1 tbsp. of soy sauce.
- 6 chicken legs.
- 1 tbsp. of ketchup.

- 1 tbsp. of Tabasco sauce.
- 1 tbsp. of cider vinegar.

Instructions:

1. Trim the tips of the drumsticks and cut halfway into the joint, linking each leg's thigh and drumstick.

2. In a tray, mix ketchup, soy sauce, vinegar, Tabasco, and roll chicken legs in the marinade.

3. Cook for about 10 minutes, skin side down, on the rack of a hot grill about 10 inches from the blaze. Cook for around 10 minutes on the other side after flipping the wings. Cook them for another 10 minutes with the skin side down.

4. Remove the legs from the heat and put them aside to rest for 5 minutes before eating.

4.7   JALAPEÑO STUFFED GAME HENS

Ready in about: 45 minutes Servings: 4 - Difficulty: moderate

Ingredients:

- Salt and freshly ground pepper to taste.

- 6 slices of bacon.

- 2 Cornish game hens.

- 4 jalapeños, halved and seeded.

Instructions:

1. Heat a grill until it is really hot.

2. Season the hens with pepper and salt before serving. Place 4 jalapeño halves in each hen's cavity. Wrap 3 slices of bacon over each hen's breast, securing the bacon with toothpicks submerged in water.

3. Place the hens on the grill and cook for around 10 minutes, or until well browned on all sides.

4. Cover grill and cook for around 40 minutes, rotating once, until hens are cooked through.

5. Remove toothpicks, cut hens lengthwise in half, divide across 4 dishes, and serve right away.

CHAPTER
06

MEAT
RECIPES

CHAPTER 5 - MEAT RECIPES

5.1 GREMLIN GRILL'S PRIME RIB

Ready in about: 3 hours and 30 minutes, plus overnight refrigeration - Servings: 10 to 14-

Difficulty: hard

Ingredients:

For Greek seasoning blend:

2 tsp. of dried oregano.

1 ½ tsp. of garlic powder.

1 tsp. of freshly ground black pepper.

1 tsp. of dried parsley flakes.

½ tsp. of ground nutmeg.

1 tsp. of salt.

1 ½ tsp. of onion powder.

1 tsp. of cornstarch.

1 tsp. of beef-flavored bouillon granules.

½ tsp. of ground cinnamon.

For rib:

- 1 cup of cherry coke.
- 1 tbsp. of kosher salt.
- Greek seasoning blend.
- 1 tsp. of dried thyme.
- 1 cup of olive oil.
- 2 tbsp. of Worcestershire sauce.
- 1 tbsp. of ground black pepper.
- 1 tbsp. of dried oregano.
- 1 tsp. of onion powder.

- 10 lb. of boneless prime rib.
- 2 tbsp. of minced garlic.

Instructions:

For Greek seasoning blend:

1. In a mixing bowl, combine all ingredients and put them in an air-tight jar. Keep in a dry place.

For rib:

1. Mix olive oil, salt, cherry coke, Worcestershire sauce, pepper, and 1 tbsp. of Greek seasoning blend in a mixing bowl.

2. Combine oregano, onion powder, thyme, and garlic in a large mixing bowl. Mix well. In a big roasting pan, place the meat. Add the marinade and rub it into the meat, rotating it to evenly cover it. Seal well the meat and marinade in an extra-large Ziploc plastic bag. Refrigerate for a day.

3. To start, create a charcoal fire. Cover the grill and place the grill rack over the coals.

4. Add the meat to a big disposable aluminum roasting pan with tiny gaps. Place the pan over the grill's center, cover it, and change the airflow, so it's partially accessible. Insert a thermometer through a ventilation hole in the grill cover to verify the temperature, which should be about 225° F. To keep the temperature in check, adjust the ventilation.

5. Cook for 2 hours and 30 minutes to 3 hours, or before an instant-read thermometer placed in the middle reads 130° F. Add coals on either side of the fire every 30 minutes or as needed to keep it burning. To keep the fire burning, add more wet wood chips as needed.

6. Remove the meat from the pan and cover it in foil. Enable for room temperature before refrigerating for at least 2 to 3 hours or overnight.

7. Light a charcoal fire to serve. Scatter the white coal over the rim of the grill. Remove inch-thick steaks from the meat and season to taste with the remaining Greek seasoning blend. Grill until done to your liking. Serve right away.

5.2   BARBECUED STEAK AU POIVRE

Ready in about: 1 hour - Servings: 6 to 10 - Difficulty: moderate

Ingredients:

- 1 tbsp. of coarse salt.

- ¼ cup of finely chopped shallots.

- 3 (1 ½-lb.) boneless shell steaks, trimmed.

- ¼ cup of crushed black peppercorns.

- ½ cup of dry red wine.

- 4 tbsp. (half stick) of non-salted butter.

- ½ cup of beef stock, home-made or canned.

Instructions:

1. Coarsely salt the steaks. Place crushed peppercorns on the surface and coat steaks on all sides with them.

2. Grill the steaks for a total of 20 minutes. Cook for about 4 minutes on one side, then flip and cook the other side for another 4 minutes. Standing steaks on their sides for many minutes can even sear the smooth rim. Continue spinning until the steaks are cooked to your taste.

3. When the steaks are grilling, mix shallot, red wine, and beef stock in a saucepan. Reduce to 1/3 of the initial volume over medium-high temperature. Transfer the cooked steaks to a serving platter that is still soft. Pour the sauce over the steaks after swirling in the fat. In a platter, slice the steaks on the bias, enabling the juices to blend with the sauce.

5.3   GRILLED FLANK STEAK

Ready in about: 15 minutes plus 2 hours refrigeration - Servings: 6 - Difficulty: moderate

Ingredients:

- ½ cup bourbon.
- ½ cup soy sauce.
- 1 ½-lb. of flank steak.

Instructions:

1. To create a marinade, add soy sauce, bourbon, and ½ a cup of water in a small bowl. Fill a gallon-size self-sealing food storage bag halfway with marinade. Place the steak in the bag and spin it many times to cover the whole cut. Marinate for 2 hours in the refrigerator, rotating the steak once after 1 hour. Remove the steak from the marinade and wipe it dry with paper towels.

2. Make a fire in the grill. Grill steak for 4 minutes on one side for rare, 5 minutes for medium-rare until flames have died down and coals are glowing. Turn the steak and cook for another 3 or 4 minutes, or until done to your liking.

3. Transfer the steak to a cutting board, cover with tape, and set aside for 5 minutes to rest. Using a sharp knife, cut the steak crosswise into 1/8-inch-thick strips.

5.4 PORTERHOUSE WITH SUMMER AU POIVRE SAUCE

Ready in about: 1 hour - Servings: 2 to 3 - Difficulty: hard

Ingredients:

- 2 tbsp. of drained pickled green peppercorns.

- ½ cup of mint leaves.

- Vegetable oil (for the grill).

- ½ cup of basil leaves.

- ½ cup of extra-virgin olive oil.

- 12 lb. porterhouse steak (about 2-inch thick).

- Kosher salt.

Instructions:

1. Prepare a grill for strong indirect heat; spray the grate with vegetable oil. Chop 2 tsp. peppercorns, then basil and mint, coarsely chopped on top of peppercorns. Add the olive oil to a small bowl and season with salt. Set aside a couple more peppercorns, coarsely sliced, for serving.

2. Season the steak with salt and pepper. Grill for 6 to 8 minutes over direct fire, turning steak every 1 minute or 2 to monitor flare-ups and ensure even browning (including standing it on its side with tongs to render and brown fat around edges) until thoroughly browned on all sides (including standing it on its side with tongs to render and brown fat around edges).

3. Grill, turning every 1 to 2 minutes and going closer to or farther away from the heat if required to create even color before an instant-read thermometer inserted into the thickest part of the steak registers 120° F for medium-rare, 10 to 12 minutes (keep tenderloin side away from heat). Allow 15 to 30 minutes to settle on a wire rack spread over a rimmed baking sheet.

4. Cut the meat out from either side of the bone on a cutting board, and slice crosswise. Serve with the sauce and the peppercorns that were saved.

5.5 HASSELBACK SHORT RIB BULGOGI

Ready in about: 40 minutes plus marinating and refrigerating time - Servings: 4 - Difficulty: easy

Ingredients:

For ssamjang:

- ¼ cup of white miso.

- 1 tsp. of sugar.

- 1 tsp. of toasted sesame seeds.

- 1 very finely chopped scallion.

- 1 tsp. of gochujang or the hot chili sauce.

- 1 tsp. of sesame oil.

For scallion salad:

- 2 tsp. of sesame oil.

- 1 tsp. of toasted sesame seeds.

- 6 scallions.

- 2 tsp. of non-seasoned rice vinegar.

For short ribs:

- 2 finely grated garlic cloves.

- 2 tbsp. of unseasoned rice vinegar.

- 1 tbsp. gochugaru or 1 tsp. of crushed red pepper flakes.

- 1 ½ lb. one-inch-thick beef short ribs.

- 1 one-inch piece of finely grated ginger.

-

- ¼ cup of soy sauce.

- 2 tbsp. of light or dark brown sugar.

- 1 tbsp. toasted sesame oil.

- Vegetable oil.

- Lettuce leaves.

- Kosher salt.

Instructions:

For the ssamjang:

1. In a small cup, combine the scallion, gochujang, miso, sugar, sesame seeds, oil, and 1 tsp. of water.

For scallion's salad:

1. Scallions should be trimmed. Cut crosswise into three-inch lengths, then slice lengthwise into matchsticks as thinly as possible. Drain well, and then pat it dry after rinsing with cold water. Toss the scallions with the vinegar, oil, and sesame seeds in a medium mixing cup.

For short ribs

1. In a medium mixing dish, add the garlic, ginger, soy sauce, brown sugar, vinegar, gochugaru, and sesame oil.

2. Slice short ribs at a steep angle per a quarter-inch with a sharp knife, cutting little more than halfway into the beef. Turn the slicer over and repeat the process, on the other side, keeping the same angle as the first. Toss the meat with the marinade in the bowl, working the marinade through the slashes in the meat. Cover the bowl with a wide plate and set it aside for at least 2 hours or up to 1 day at room temperature.

3. Prepare your grill for medium-high temperature with vegetable oil on the grate. Remove the short ribs from the marinade and season them gently with salt. Grill, rotating every 2 minutes and switch to a cooler section of the grill if necessary, until the meat is solid to the touch and a streak of pink can be seen peeking inside the deepest slashes, 10 minutes.

4. Transfer the short ribs to a chopping board and set aside for at least 5 minutes before chopping through the slashes.

5. Season the scallion salad with salt. Serve the short ribs with ssamjang and scallion salad, if needed, covered in lettuce.

5.6 LACQUERED RIB EYE

Ready in about: 1 hour plus marinating and refrigerating time - Servings: 2 to 4 - Difficulty: hard

Ingredients:

- 2 tbsp. of soy sauce.

- 2 tsp. of sugar.

- Vegetable oil.

- Kosher salt.

- ¼ cup of red wine vinegar or sherry vinegar.

- 1 tbsp. of fish sauce.

- 1 crushed garlic clove.

- Flaky sea salt.

- 2 ½ lb. rib eye.

- Extra-virgin olive oil.

- Lemon wedges.

Instructions:

1. In a shallow saucepan over medium-high heat, bring the soy sauce, vinegar, sugar, fish sauce, and garlic to a simmer. Lower the heat to low and slowly boil for around 7 to 8 minutes, or until the liquid has been decreased by around half. Set aside the sauce.

2. Prepare your grill; spray the grate with oil. Season the steak with pepper and kosher salt. Afterward, grill for around 8 to 9 minutes, rotating every minute over direct heat until thoroughly charred on all sides.

3. Cook the steak over indirect heat, rotating every 2 minutes and shifting closer to or further away from the heat if required to obtain even color, for around 15 minutes, or for the time when a thermometer inserted into the thickest part of the steak shows 100° F. Begin basting the beef. Continue to barbecue, turning and basting with a slight coating of the sauce as required to produce a deep crust on the steak, until its brown and thermometer registers 120° F for medium-rare texture, for about 10 to 12 minutes. Allow 30 minutes for the steak to sit on a wired rack.

4. Break the steak into thick slices on a chopping board. Arrange on a plate and drizzle it with the olive oil before seasoning with. Serve with the wedges of lemon on the side.

5.7 BULGOGI (KOREAN BARBECUED BEEF)

Ready in about: 20 minutes - Servings: 6 to 8 - Difficulty: easy

Ingredients:

- 3 ½ tbsp. of soy sauce.

- 5 tbsp. of scallions, chopped on the diagonal.

- 1 ½ tbsp. of toasted crushed sesame seeds.

- 2 tbsp. of sesame oil.

- 1 ½ lb. beef tenderloin or flank steak.

- 1 ½ tbsp. of sugar.

- 1 tsp. of minced garlic.

- 1 large thinly sliced onion.

- 2 tbsp. of rice wine.

- 2 tbsp. of sherry.

- ¼ tsp. of black pepper.

Instructions:

1. Cut the beef into one-and-a-half-inch squares that are 1/8 inches thick. It's easier to thinly dice the beef because it's partially frozen.

2. Combine the beef and the remaining components in a mixing bowl.

3. Over a charcoal fire, grill all of the beef and onion slices until they are just brown on the outside and pink on the inside. It will take 2 to 4 minutes to complete this task.

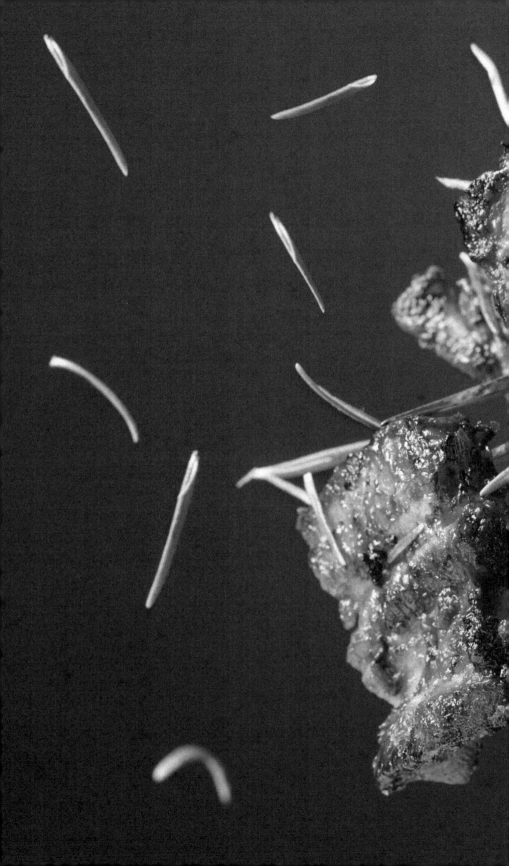

CHAPTER 07

PORK RECIPES

CHAPTER 6 - PORK RECIPES

6.1 GRILLED PORK CHOPS WITH FRIED SAGE LEAVES

Ready in about: 10 minutes - Servings: 4 - Difficulty: easy

Ingredients:

- Juice of 1 lemon.

- 2 tbsp. of olive oil.

- About ½ cup vegetable oil (enough for half an inch in the pan).

- 4 loin pork chops.

- 1 minced clove of garlic.

- Coarse salt and freshly ground pepper to taste.

- 30 fresh sage leaves.

Instructions:

1. Combine garlic, lemon juice, and olive oil in a bowl and coat pork chops. Enable 30 minutes to marinate at room temperature. Season with pepper and salt and grill for around 20 minutes or until cooked through, rotating once over hot coals.

2. Heat the vegetable oil in a skillet and fry the sage leaves for around 2 minutes, or until crisp. Drain on paper towels after removing using a slotted spoon.

3. Serve pork chops with sage leaves as a garnish.

6.2 NORTH CAROLINA-STYLE PULLED PORK

Ready in about: 5 to 7 hours - Servings: 10 to 12 - Difficulty: hard

Ingredients:

For pork:

- ¼ cup of basic rub for barbecue.

- 1 bone-in pork shoulder roast (5 to 6 lb.).

- 4 cups of hickory chips, soaked in cold water for 1 hour and then drained.

For the vinegar sauce:

- 2 tbsp. of sugar, or to taste.

- 1 ½ cups of cider vinegar.

- 1 tbsp. of red pepper flakes.

- ½ tsp. of freshly ground black pepper.

- 2 tsp. of salt, or to taste.

Instructions:

1. Preheat the grill to 325° F. If using wood, create a fire on opposite sides of the grill; if using gas, build a fire on one side or opposite sides of the grill. Rub the rub all over the bacon.

2. While utilizing charcoal, apply fresh coals and half cup wood chips to each mound of coals every hour for the first 4 hours. Place wood chips in the smoker box if using coal, and preheat before smoke appears.

3. Place the pork fat side up on the barbecue, away from the flames, over the drip tray. Grill for 4 to 6 hours, or until the beef is nicely browned and cooked through, or until the internal temperature reaches 195° F.

4. Meanwhile, whisk together the ingredients for the vinegar sauce in a bowl of 3/4 cup sugar. If required, season with more salt or sugar to taste.

5. Transfer the fried pork to a cutting board, cover with tape, and set aside for 15 minutes or until cool enough to touch. Remove all flesh, bones, or fat from the meat and discard. Pull each slice of pork into shreds about 2 inches long by 14 inches wide with your fingertips or a fork. (Alternatively, use a cleaver to finely cut the meat.) Pour 1 cup vinegar sauce, or sufficiently to hold the meat moist and juicy, into a metal or foil jar. Cover with foil and remain warm on the barbecue before ready to eat. Serve with coleslaw and the leftover sauce on the hamburger buns.

6.3   GRILLED PORK PORTERHOUSE WITH AN APPLE-MAPLE-GINGER SAUCE

Ready in about: 30 minutes plus refrigeration - Servings: 6 - Difficulty: hard

Ingredients:

For the brine:

- 5 tbsp. of kosher salt.

- 3 tbsp. of crushed garlic.

- 3⁄4 cup onion slices, cut into 1⁄4-inch-thick rings.

- 1⁄4 cup of maple syrup.

- 3 tbsp. of sliced peeled fresh ginger.

- 1 sprig of fresh sage.

- 5 bay leaves.

- 6 (1 1⁄4-inch-thick) pork loin chops.

- 2 tsp. of peppercorns.

For the infused oil:

- 1 bay leaf.
- 2 tbsp. of minced shallot.
- 1 tbsp. of coriander seeds.
- 1 tbsp. of peppercorns.

- 1 tsp. of minced fresh thyme.
- 1⁄2 cup of vegetable oil.
- 1 tsp. of minced fresh rosemary.

For the sauce:

- 1⁄4 cup of minced shallot.

- 2 cups of apple juice.

- Three-star anise.

- 1⁄2 cup of maple syrup.

- 2 tbsp. of butter.

- 1 tbsp. of minced garlic.

- ½ cup of chicken stock.

- 2 tbsp. of minced fresh ginger.

- ½ vanilla bean, seeds scraped.

- Salt and freshly ground black pepper to taste.

- 1 tbsp. of agar.

Instructions:

1. Stir all of the brine ingredients except pork into 1-quart water in a big pot and bring to a boil 24 hours before cooking. Allow cooling to room temperature before serving. Refrigerate pork chops after submerging them in brine.

2. Prepare the flavored oil the next morning by grinding bay leaf, coriander, and peppercorns in a spice mill or a clean coffee grinder, then mixing with the remaining ingredients in a medium cup. Enable to cool to room temperature.

3. To make the sauce, first, melt butter in a saucepan over a medium-low flame. Add the shallot and cook for 4 minutes, or until caramelized. Cook for 1 minute after adding the garlic. Apple juice, star anise, chicken stock, and ginger are applied to the pot. Bring to a boil, then limit to ¼ of its original volume. Simmer for 3 minutes with vanilla pod maple syrup, and seeds, and agar.

4. Remove the pan from the sun. Drop the vanilla pod and star anise. In a blender or food processor, puree the paste, then strain it into a jar via a fine-mesh sieve. Season with salt and pepper to taste.

5. Heat a charcoal or gas grill to medium-high temperatures. Clean the meat by rinsing it and patting it dry with paper towels; after brushing the chops with the flavored oil, season gently with salt. Grill to medium doneness, around 6 minutes per foot, or until internal temperature hits 135° F to 140° F on a thermometer and center is light pink. Allow for a 5-minute rest before serving. Serve with a warm sauce drizzled on top.

6.4   BBQ PORK TENDERLOIN

Ready in about: 1 hour and 40 minutes plus marinating and refrig-erating time - Servings: 4 to 6 - Difficulty: hard

Ingredients:

- 2 cups of chopped onions.

- ½ cup of soy sauce.

- ¼ cup of sugar.

- 4 minced cloves of garlic.

- ½ cup of fresh lemon juice.

- ½ cup of corn oil.

- 3 to 4 tbsp. of ground cori-ander.

- 6 pork tenderloins.

- Tabasco sauce.

Instructions:

1. Stir together lemon juice, garlic, onions, oil, soy sauce, coriander, sugar, and Tabasco sauce in a large mixing cup.

2. Place entire tenderloins in the marinade and then set them aside in the refrigerator for around 5 to 6 hours.

3. Set the grill about 5 inches above the heat.

4. Remove the meat from the marinade, transfer the marinade to a frying pan and keep it warm as the meat heats.

5. Place tenderloins on the grill, leaving enough room between them to spin. Turn the parts after around 30 minutes and spoon the marinade over them; repeat on the other side. Grill for about 1 hour.

6. Spread cooked marinade over each tenderloin before eating.

6.5 GRILLED PORK LOIN WITH WINE-SALT RUB

Ready in about: 2 hours 30 minutes plus marinating time - Servings: 8 to 10 - Difficulty: hard

Ingredients:

- ¾ cup of coarse sea salt.

- 2 strips of finely chopped lemon zest.

- 1 (about 3 ½-lb.) boneless pork loin.

- 2 cups of fruity white wine,

such as riesling or gewürztraminer.

- 8 sprigs of fresh thyme leaves stripped (about 2 tbsp. of leaves).

- 1 cup of sugar.

Instructions:

1. Reduce wine by half in a medium heavy-bottomed pan over medium heat for 30 minutes; reduce heat to low and proceed to cook down to 2 tsp. Enable to cool absolutely.

2. Combine the salt, lemon zest, thyme leaves, and wine reduction in a food processor. Process 2 or 3 times. Add the sugar and pulse once more before the mixture resembles moist powder. If the mixture is stickier, spread it out uniformly on a sheet pan and set it aside for some hours or for overnight.

3. Put the pork in a baking tray. Using a half cup of salt rub, rub the pork all over. Refrigerate for at least 3 to 4 hours or for overnight, securely wrapped in plastic wrap.

4. Light your grill for indirect high-heat cooking by stacking charcoal on 1 side and keeping the other unlit. To collect some drips, put a piece of foil or a disposable metal roasting pan below the grill on the unlit side. Place the pork over the foil on the barbecue. Cover the grill and cook for 1 hour to 90 minutes, turn it every 30 minutes until meat hits 140° F in the middle. Allow 10 minutes to rest before slicing it.

6.6 GRILLED PORK SHOULDER STEAKS WITH HERB SALAD

Ready in about: 40 minutes plus marinating time - Servings: 8 - Difficulty: hard

Ingredients:

- 6 garlic cloves.

- ⅓ cup plus 3 tbsp. of fresh lime juice.

- 8 ¾-inch thick pork shoulder steaks.

- 3 cups of Thai or sweet basil leaves, Dill or cilantro leaves.

- 4 medium shallots.

- ⅓ cup plus 3 tbsp. of fish sauce.

- 3 tbsp. of light brown sugar.

- 2 thinly sliced red or green Thai chilies.

- A pinch of salt and pepper.

Instructions:

1. In a mixer, combine minced shallots, garlic, ⅓ cup of fish sauce, ⅓ cup of lime juice, and 2 tsp. brown sugar until creamy.

2. Season steaks with a pinch of salt and pepper. Place in a big mixing bowl or a 12x9 inches baking dish to cool. Pour the marinade over the steaks and transform them with tongs to cover them properly. Allow to stay for 1 hour at room temperature, or cover and chill for up to 12 hours, turning once (halfway through if you can).

3. Preheat your grill to high. 7 to 9 minutes on the grill, rotating steaks every minute or 2 until gently charred and crisp, and an instant-read thermometer inserted into the thickest portion registers 140° F. Place the steaks on a cutting board and set aside for at least 5 minutes before slicing thinly.

4. In a big mixing bowl, combine the chilies, the remaining 3 tbsp. of fish sauce, the remaining 3 tbsp. of lime juice, the remaining 1 tbsp. of brown sugar, and 1tbsp. of water. Toss in the cut shallots and spices, seasoning gently with salt.

5. Arrange the sliced meat on a platter and top it with the herb salad.

6.7 SPICY PORK SKEWERS

Ready in about: 40 minutes plus marinating time - Servings: 8 - Difficulty: hard

Ingredients:

- Half small red onion, thinly sliced.

- 8 garlic cloves, coarsely chopped.

- ½ cup of soy sauce.

- ¼ cup of sugar.

- 1 tbsp. of kosher salt, plus more.

- 2 lb. skinless, boneless pork shoulder.

- 12 red Thai chilies, coarsely chopped.

- 1 cup of Sprite or 7UP.

- ⅓ cup cane vinegar (such as Datu Puti) or unseasoned rice vinegar.

- 1 tbsp. of black peppercorns.

- 6 dried shiitake mushrooms.

Instructions:

1. Freeze pork on a rimmed baking sheet for 45 to 60 minutes or until really solid around the edges. Take the pork from the fridge and thinly slice it. Using a sharp knife, break the bits lengthwise into 1"–2" short strips.

2. In a big resealable plastic container, add the onion, garlic, chilies, Sprite, vinegar, sugar, soy sauce, peppercorns, and 1 tsp. salt. Mushrooms, ground to a powder in a spice mill or mortar and pestle, are whisked onto the marinade. Apply a few bits of pork at a time, covering thoroughly so they don't cling together and can consume the marinade equally. Chill for 6 to 8 hours, covered.

3. Preheat the grill to medium-high. Remove the pork from the marinade and skewer it. Bring the marinade to a boil in a shallow saucepan over high heat on the barbecue. Cook for 1 minute, skimming any foam that grows to the tip. Transfer to a cooler portion of the barbecue.

4. Season pork lightly with salt and roast, uncovered, for 2 minutes or until well browned. Switch the beef over and baste with the marinade. Continue to barbecue, rotating and basting every minute, for another 4 minutes or until the chicken is cooked through and browned all over.

CHAPTER 7 - SEAFOOD RECIPES

7.1 CHARCOAL-GRILLED STRIPED BASS

Ready in about: 45 minutes - Servings: 4 to 8 - Difficulty: moderate

Ingredients:

- Salt and freshly ground black pepper.

- 1 large sprig of fresh rosemary.

- Oil.

- 1 (3-to 4-lb.) striped bass, gutted.

- 1 peeled clove of garlic.

- 1 bay leaf.

- ¼-lb. of (1 stick) butter, melted and kept hot.

- Lemon wedges.

- ¼ cup of chopped fresh parsley.

Instructions:

1. Construct a charcoal fire. They're ready as white ash forms on top of the coals.

2. Prepare the fish in the meantime. Salt and pepper, it both inside and out. Using a knife, shave a garlic clove into slivers. Create a few small incisions around the backbone of the fish using a thin paring knife. Garlic slivers can be included.

3. In the cavity of the fish, place a rosemary sprig and a bay leaf. To protect the cavity, tie the fish in 2 or 3 positions with thread. Using a generous quantity of oil, massage the fish all over. Put the fish on a hot grill and cook for 10 to 15 minutes; brush with butter if desired.

4. Remove the fish from the grill with a pancake turner, spatula, or both and flip it. Cook for a further 10 to 15 minutes on that side, or until the fish is cooked through and the meat flakes easily when examined with a fork. Cooking time is defined by the size of the fish, the temperature of the heat, and the proximity of the fish to the coals.

5. Place the fish on a hot platter and drizzle with the remaining butter. Add parsley and lemon wedges for a finishing touch.

7.2 WHITE FISH FILLETS WITH GRILLED CABBAGE

Ready in about: 45 minutes - Servings: 2 to 4 - Difficulty: moderate

Ingredients:

- 4 savoy cabbage leaves.

- 4 tsp. of chopped fresh dill.

- Olive oil as needed.

- 2 tbsp. of butter.

- 1 meaty skeleton from a small white fish, like sea bass, chopped.

- Microgreens or flowers for garnish.

- Salt for cabbage.

- 8 oz. of skinless white-fish fillets, cut into 4 small pieces.

- Salt and black pepper as per your taste.

- 1 tbsp. of neutral oil (like grapeseed or corn).

- Several sprigs of fresh thyme.

- 2 cups dry white wine.

Instructions:

1. Heat a grill with the rack next to the flame, and really nice.

2. Bring a big pot of salted water to a boil. Remove the thickest section of each cabbage leaf's central vein without slicing the leaf in half. Blanch cabbage leaves in boiling water for 30 seconds or until only tender; drain on paper towels. Place a slice of fish on one side of each leaf and top with 1 tsp. dill, salt and pepper, and a drizzle of olive oil. To make an oval, fold the other half of the leaf over the fish and trim the edges with a large cookie cutter or a knife. Apply a small amount of olive oil to the exterior.

3. In a skillet wide enough to keep fish bones in one layer, heat neutral oil and 1 tbsp. butter over medium-high heat; when the butter melts, add thyme and fish bones and fry, stirring periodically, until very well browned around 5 minutes. Cook, sometimes stirring, until the remaining 1 tbsp. of butter has melted and the wine has decreased in amount, around 10 minutes. Remove the bones from the fish and discard them. Season the sauce with salt and pepper and hold it warm as you cook the fish.

4. Grill the fish packets for 30 seconds on either side; the cabbage should brown, and the fish should scarcely steam.

5. To foam up the sauce, whisk it or use an immersion blender. Serve by drizzling sauce over cabbage and fish and garnishing with microgreens or flowers.

SEAFOOD RECIPES

7.3 STEPHAN PYLES'S GRILLED REDFISH WITH SMOKED TOMATO SALSA AND BLACK-EYED PEAS–JICAMA RELISH

Ready in about: 10 minutes - Servings: 4 - Difficulty: easy

Ingredients:

For the black-eyed pea–jicama relish:

- 1 ½ cups of fish or chicken stock.

- 1 tbsp. of each diced red and yellow bell pepper.

- 1 small serrano chili, seeded and minced.

- 3 tbsp. of diced mango, papaya, or cantaloupe.

- Salt to taste.

- 6 tbsp. of dried black-eyed peas.

- 2 oz. of jicama, peeled and cut into small, ¼-inch pieces.

- 1 tbsp. of diced sweet onion.

- 2 tbsp. of diced cucumber.

- 1 tsp. of finely chopped fresh spearmint.

For the smoked tomato salsa:

- 1 tbsp. of extra virgin olive oil.

- 3 medium-size scallions, including white and green parts, diced.

- ½ cup fresh cilantro leaves, finely chopped.

- Salt and freshly ground black pepper to taste.

- 4 small (about 1 lb.) very ripe tomatoes.

- 2 tbsp. of each diced green, red and yellow bell pepper.

- 3 small serrano chilies, seeded and diced.

- Salt and freshly ground black pepper to taste.

- 4 (6-oz.) redfish fillets.

- 2 tbsp. of tasteless vegetable oil or clarified butter.

Instructions:

1. 1 hour before serving, render the black-eyed pea relish. Soak black-eyed peas in warm water for 20 to 30 minutes, or until they are soft and have grown marginally in bulk. Bring them to a boil in fish or chicken stock and simmer for 20 minutes, or until tender but always crisp. In a medium-size mixing dish, combine peas and remaining relish ingredients. Season with salt to taste and properly combine.

2. To smoke the tomatoes, firstly build and light a fire in a grill, preferably with hardwood charcoal briquettes. 6 to 8 aromatic wood chunks or 4 cups of wood chips can be soaked in warm water for 20 minutes.

3. After around 20 minutes, when the briquettes are glowing but mildly grey, apply the soaked wood chunks and let them flame for 5 minutes.

4. Tomatoes can be put on the grill. Cover the grill and smoke the tomatoes for 10 minutes before cutting them. Set aside the tomatoes after they have been peeled, seeded, and diced.

5. To sustain a hot fire with lots of red coals, add ample charcoal to the barbecue.

6. In a big skillet, melt the olive oil over medium-high heat to produce the smoked tomato sauce. Cook until the scallions, peppers, and serrano chilies are slightly tender around 3 minutes. Stir in the smoked tomatoes and cilantro, then season with salt and pepper to match. Takedown from the heat and put aside to stay warm.

7. To grill the snapper, spray either side with oil and cook for 4 minutes on either side on the barbecue or until opaque but always offering somewhat, not too soft or too rough. Add salt and freshly ground pepper as per the taste.

8. Divide the smoked tomato sauce equally among 4 warmed dinner plates to eat. Place a snapper fillet on top of the sauce and spoon-relish over it in a diagonal line. Serve right away.

7.4 GRILLED SNAPPER WITH CUMIN

Ready in about: 40 minutes - Servings: 4 - Difficulty: moderate

Ingredients:

- Vegetable oil.

- 4 (9-to 12-oz.) rose thorn snappers or 2 (1-to 2-lb.) Alaska red snappers or red-fish, cleaned, heads on.

- ½ tsp. of cumin seeds.

- Kosher or coarse sea salt to taste.

- 4 tbsp. plus 2 tsp. of olive oil.

Instructions:

1. Clean the fish by rinsing it and patting it dry. Keep it refrigerated before you're able to use it.

2. In an outdoor grill, create and light a fire.

3. Preheat the oven to 300ª F.

4. When the coals are bright red and evenly dusted with dirt, use cooking oil and paper towels to properly oil the barbecue.

5. Cut 4 1/8-inch-deep holes through either side of each fish when the fire is blazing, using a very sharp knife blade to create cuts through the scales of the fish. Similar volumes of cumin seed (15 seeds is the optimum amount) should be tightly pressed into the cuts.

6. 2 tsp. of olive oil should be rubbed all over each trout. Place the fish on the grill such that the rungs are vertical under the fish's body. Cook for no more than 3 minutes per side for a small fish, 4 to 5 minutes for a big fish, or until golden grill marks appear.

7. Move fish to an oven-proof dish or baking sheet coated with foil with a finely oiled metal spatula and continue cooking in the oven until opaque within 8 to 10 minutes for a small fish, 15 to 20 minutes for a larger one. Stick the tip of a sharp knife through the meat just below the fish's head and pull out and see if it's cooked. It's best if the beef is translucent.

8. Place the remaining 4 tbsp. of olive oil in a flame-proof dish or ramekin and place it in the oven to heat gently around 5 minutes until the fish is done.

9. Place each fish in the middle of a dinner plate to eat. Pour 1 tbsp. of warm olive oil on 1 side of the fish and a thin strip of coarse salt on the other. Remove fillets from larger fish and put equal-sized pieces of fillet on each plate, seasoning with salt and oil. Serve right away.

7.5   GRILLED SWORDFISH STEAKS WITH ORANGE THYME SAUCE

Ready in about: 30 minutes - Servings: 4 - Difficulty: moderate

Ingredients:

- 3 tbsp. of olive oil.

- 1 minced shallot.

- 2 medium-ripe tomatoes, chopped.

- 2/3 cup of fresh orange juice.

- Salt and ground pepper according to taste.

- 2 swordfish steaks (about 2 to 2 ½ lb. in all).

- 2 tbsp. of unsalted butter.

- 1 minced clove of garlic.

- ¼ cup of fresh thyme leaves.

- ¼ cup to half cup dry white wine.

Instructions:

1. Using paper towels rinse swordfish steaks. Using 2 tsp. of olive oil, coat all sides of the chicken.

2. In a pan with 1 tbsp. of butter, heat the remaining 1 tbsp. of olive oil. Cook until the garlic and shallots are tender. Cook for 3 minutes after adding the thyme and tomatoes.

3. Cook for 5 minutes more after adding the white wine and orange juice. Season the fish with pepper and salt and put aside until ready to cook.

4. Preheat the grill. Cook for 5 minutes on either side. In the meantime, put the sauce to a boil. Remove the pan from the heat and whisk the leftover 1 tbsp. of butter. Serve the steaks with the sauce

7.6 GRILLED SARDINES

Ready in about: 30 minutes - Servings: 4 - Difficulty: moderate

Ingredients:

- 2 tbsp. of extra virgin olive oil.

- 24 medium or large sardines, cleaned.

- Salt and freshly ground pepper.

- Lemon wedges.

- A handful of sprigs of fresh rosemary.

Instructions:

1. Prepare a hot grill and make sure it's properly oiled. Sardines can be rinsed and dried with paper towels. Season with salt and pepper after tossing with olive oil.

2. Toss rosemary sprigs directly on the fire until the grill is primed. If required, wait for the flames to die down before placing sardines directly overheating in batches. Depending on distance, grill for 1 minute or 2 on either foot. Using tongs or a large metal spatula, move to a platter and serve with lemon wedges.

7.7 GINGER AND CHILI GRILLED SHRIMP

Ready in about: 1 hour and 15 minutes - Servings: 6 - Difficulty: moderate

Ingredients:

- 1 tbsp. of grated fresh ginger.

- 2 crushed cloves of garlic.

- ½ tsp. of freshly ground black pepper.

- ½ cup of low-fat buttermilk.

- 2 minced jalapeños.

- 1 tsp. of Kosher salt.

- 18 jumbo shrimp peeled and deveined, tails left on.

- 1 small lime, cut into 6 wedges.

- 2 ripe mangos, peeled, seeded, and cut into 1-inch dice.

Instructions:

1. In a medium mixing dish, combine buttermilk, ginger, jalapeños, salt, garlic, and pepper. To mix the ingredients, whisk them together. Toss in the shrimp and coat properly with a wooden spoon. Refrigerate for 1 hour to marinate.

2. Soak 6 wooden skewers for 10 minutes in hot. Alternating shrimp and mango, thread 3 shrimp and 2 mango bits into each skewer.

3. In the grill, start a fire. Grill shrimp for 4 to 6 minutes on either side until invisible, until the flames have died down and the coals are glowing. A wedge of lime should be served with each skewer.

CHAPTER 8 - CONCLUSION

We'd have to cook with less heat and lose taste if we didn't have the grill's searing high heat. Caramelization happens as proteins and sugars experience a transformation as a consequence of a chemical reaction that allows food to caramel as it heats. This gives grilled meats and vegetables a delicious increase of scent and taste. Consider marshmallows, caramelized onions, and, of course, the beef. They all taste ten times better when grilled.

Grilled food is simple, yet exotic food and the go-to food of every generation in the present world. Either the eldest member of the community or the youngest, everyone craves the grilled food.

This book covered a wide variety of grilling recipes that you can try at home with ease and become a pro at grilling.

Grilled food has its own benefits. This method of cooking lets you cook the food on direct heat in less amount of time and thus preserve the vital nutrients of the food. It is a technique that is age-old and is being followed since the very origin of the fire.

In this book, simple recipes were covered and you can easily try them at home. So, keep grilling.

Thank you and good luck!